A Pirate Alphabet

The ABCs

of Piracy!

by Anna Butzer

illustrated by Chris Jevons

PICTURE WINDOW BOOKS

a capstone imprint

A is for adventure.

Sailing the high seas, visiting secret islands, and finding buried treasure—pirates had their fair share of adventure!

is for **bounty.**

A bounty was a reward given for the capture of a pirate. In the eyes of pirates, a high bounty was a sign of strength. It meant that people saw them as a threat.

BOUNTY

Captain Messy Beard

$2.99 Reward!

 **is for captain.**

Pirate captains did not wear flashy clothes. Captains were captured first! To avoid being captured, captains dressed like the rest of the crew.

D is for Davy Jones' Locker.

Way down deep, as deep as can be, is Davy Jones' Locker—the bottom of the sea. Davy Jones was the evil spirit of the sea. "Going to Davy Jones Locker" meant someone had died or a ship had sunk.

 **is for eye patch.**

Some pirates wore eye patches to keep one eye used to seeing in the dark. Below deck, they could flip up the patch and see right away.

F is for fight.

Pirates' lives were full of danger. They always had to be ready for a fight. They battled people on the ships they attacked. Many pirates used short swords called cutlasses.

G is for gangway.

The gangway is a passage along either side of a ship's upper deck. Pirates also yelled, "Gangway!" to get through a crowd.

is for **hook.**

A hook could be used in place of a hand. Captain Hook was even named for it in the book *Peter Pan*!

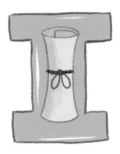

is for island.

When they weren't sailing the high seas, pirates dropped anchor on uncharted islands. Pirates might have used islands as a place to hide from the law.

No Pirates Here!

J is for Jolly Roger.

The most famous pirate flag was the Jolly Roger. When sailors saw the skull and crossbones, it always meant one thing ... pirates!

 **is for knots.**

When it comes to sailing, knots are almost as important as the wind. A poorly tied knot could threaten the safety of everyone aboard the ship.

L is for "Land ho!"

A lookout way up in the crow's nest watched for the next place to stop. If she spotted land, she yelled, "Land ho!"

land ho!

M is for marooned.

Members of the crew might be marooned as punishment if they broke a rule. They would be put ashore on an island and abandoned.

N is for navigate.

Pirates had special tools to navigate the open oceans. They used maps, charts, and compasses to know where they were.

 **is for ocean.**

Pirates have probably sailed the oceans as long as people have been sailing. Most people think of pirates during the 1600s and 1700s. Attacks were common in the Caribbean Sea and Pacific, Indian, and Atlantic Oceans.

P is for plunder.

No gold is safe if sea thieves are near. Hide the doubloons, silver, and gold! If pirates found treasure, it was plundered and sold.

SWAG

SWAG

 **is for quartermaster.**

The quartermaster was second in command on a pirate ship. He made sure the crew followed the captain's orders. The quartermaster was loyal and brave.

R is for rules.

Pirates were ruthless lawbreakers. They needed rules to help them get along. To be a part of the crew, a pirate had to agree to follow the rules.

Rules!
1. Talk like a pirate
2. Act like a pirate
3. Scrub the deck like a pirate!
4. Scrub the deck harder!
5. Eat yer greens!
6. Only parrots as pets!
7. Lights out after dinner!
8. No landlubbers!
9. Clear the deck!
10. Listen to yer Captain!
11. Plunder ye Treasure!

is for sails.

Speed was important for pirate ships. Big ships with large sails were faster than little ships with smaller sails.

T is for treasure.

Most people think pirate treasure was always gold and jewels. But many other items were valuable to pirates. They stole ropes, sails, and tools.

U is for underwater.

Going underwater meant a bad day for pirates. Today, people dive to see sunken ships and treasure from the time of pirates.

 **is for vessel.**

A pirate's vessel was a wooden ship. Pirates worked hard to keep their ship strong, safe, and speedy. Their ship was their home.

 **is for whistle.**

Pirates believed that whistling on a ship would bring stormy weather. Have you ever heard the phrase "to whistle up a storm"?

X is for X marks the spot.

Maps with an X to mark the spot probably didn't exist.
Pirates would memorize where they hid their treasure
and told only those they could trust.

Y is for "Yo ho ho!"

Pirates sang songs as they worked on their ship. These songs told tales about life as a pirate. Some of these sea songs included the words, "Yo ho ho!"

Z is for zephyr.

With a strong western wind, a ship will set sail. Across miles of ocean, a boat will be carried by a light breeze called a zephyr.

28

Glossary

abandoned—deserted or neglected

compass—an instrument people use to find the direction in which they are traveling; a compass has a needle that points north

crew—a team of people who work together

cutlass—a short sword with a curved blade

doubloon—an old gold coin of Spain and Spanish America

gloom—a dark or shadowy place

phrase—a group of words that expresses a thought but is not a complete sentence

ruthless—cruel and unconcerned about others

tale—an exciting or dramatic story

threat—someone or something that could cause harm or trouble

uncharted—unknown territory; not on a map

Read More

Bunting, Eve. *P is for Pirate: A Pirate Alphabet*. Ann Arbor, Mich.: Sleeping Bear Press, 2014.

Fliess, Sue. *How to Be a Pirate*. A Little Golden Book. New York: Golden Books, 2014.

Robinson, Michelle. *Goodnight Pirate*. Hauppage, NY: Barron's Educational Series, 2015.

Internet Sites

FactHound offers a safe, fun way to find Internet sites related to this book. All of the sites on FactHound have been researched by our staff.

Here's all you do:

Visit *www.facthound.com*

Type in this code: 9781479568864

Super-cool stuff! Check out projects, games and lots more at **www.capstonekids.com**

Index

JJ
BUTZER
ANNA

Editor: Gillia Olson
Designer: Ashlee Suker
Art Director: Nathan Gassman
Production Specialist: Katy LaVigne
The illustrations in this book were created digitally.

Picture Window Books are published by Capstone,
1710 Roe Crest Drive, North Mankato, Minnesota 56003
www.mycapstone.com

Library of Congress Cataloging-in-Publication Data
Library of Congress Cataloging-in-Publication data is available on the
Library of Congress website.

978-1-4795-6886-4 (hardcover)
978-1-4795-6914-4 (paperback)
978-1-4795-6926-7 (e-Book pdf)

Printed and bound in the United States of America.
009653F16

Other Titles in This Series

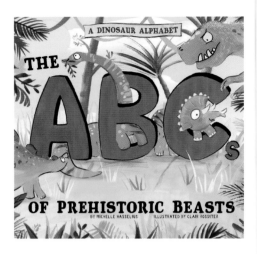